Encounters

ISBN: 978-178456-704-0

Perfect Bound

First published 2020 by UPFRONT PUBLISHING
Peterborough, England.

An environmentally friendly book printed and bound in England
by www.printondemand-worldwide.com

ENCOUNTERS

These being some of the people, books and events
that have come into my life as I celebrate the
sixtieth anniversary of my ordination

by
Kenneth Payne

Acknowledgements

I am grateful to Pat Billett for permission to publish her poem, to Anthony Weatley for details regarding Fr Dolly Brookes, OSB, to Caroline Richards for the Reflections on her husband, to Dunc Dyason regarding his work in Guatamala, to Fr Bede Griffiths for his article on age, to Fr De Mello for details of his spiritual exercises, to Clodovis Boff for the extract from his book "Feet on the ground Theology", and to Bishop Robert Barron for his comments on "The Goldfinch". However, most of all, my thanks go to Tita Lobo for her work in deciphering my scrawl and to Lorne Foort for her comments and proof-reading.

Proceeds from the sale of this book will go to the Missionaries of the Poor, (MOPSA).

Several quotations have been taken from previous books I have had published, and the following are a few further books that I found helpful and inspiring:

The books on marriage by Jack Dominion

"Alive in God" by Timothy Radcliffe. Asks the question, what does it mean to be human? Wherein lies our happiness?

"The City is my Monastery" by Richard Carter. This is an inspiring book about being caught up in the holiness of God in the down to earth life of the city.

"A Nun's Story" by Sister Agatha
On a day when Shirley Leech when writing to her fiancé about the purchase of chairs for their new home, her hand stopped writing and continued unbidden by itself: "but there's no point now, as I am going to be a nun". The story of how this happened and subsequent events in her life makes fascinating reading.

"Life beyond Death" by John Tormey

This is a short easy to read book which makes helpful reading for those who are seriously ill, those who care for them, and those who grieve. It is a warm and sympathetic book dealing with a subject that is often difficult to discuss.

"The Betrothed" by Alessandro Manzoni. This is one of Pope Francis' favourite books. It is a historical novel of love and intrigue and an excellent introduction to it is to be found in the Wikipedia

"Jo Cox – More in Common" by Brendon Cox. This is by the husband of Jo Cox, MP, whose murder in June 2016 shocked the world. Brendon gives a very moving portrait of Jo and all that she stood for. "Jo would have no regrets about her life, she lived every day of it to the full".

"Faith and Contemplation" by Rene Voillaume
"The Sacrament of the Present Moment" by Jean-Pierre Caussade
"All is Grace" by Henri Boulad
"Your God is too Small" by J.B. Phillips
"Hereafter" by David Winter
"Hope for the Flowers" by Trina Paulus

And, most important of all, the Encyclicals and Exhortations of Pope Francis.

CONTENTS

Chapter 1

Introduction

"I have come to bring fire on the earth" (Luke 12 v49)

This small book is a very personal memoir of a few of the many people who have come into my life, interspersed with a mention of various books which have interested and inspired me. More recently the list must include items which have appeared on the internet. I make no apology for repeating details of a few of the people about whom I have recently written in several other books. There are those who are well-known, some whom you may recognise, and others again, who for reasons of confidentiality must remain anonymous; but all who have had an influence on me in various, and at times, remarkable ways.

My pen, I must admit has become rather like a supermarket trolley, going everywhere but straight. However, it has caused me to ask myself: "What are my priorities and how does the Gospel infuse all that I try to do and all that I am?" One retreat master made a point that it was all summed up in trying to live in the present moment and this meant spelling out in order: sleep, exercise, prayer, time with others and work! I hope then that you, the reader, may be inspired by finding in these meanderings that, in the words of Pope Francis, "Christ is alive! He is our hope, and in a wonderful way he brings youth to our world, and everything he touches becomes young, new, full of life, and he wants you to be alive" (from "Christ Lives" by Pope Francis).

I was born in Acton, West London, in 1930, but when, at the age of five my mother became ill with tuberculosis, I was shipped off to my grandparents in the country near Burnham-on-Crouch in Essex. This whetted my appetite for the country, so that when my mother finally recovered and moved to Farnham in Surrey my enjoyment of the countryside continued.

It was at this time that the book I most enjoyed reading, many times over, was Kenneth Graham's "The Wind in the Willows". The story of Ratty and Mole, and, of course Toad, spells out so many characteristics of our own human nature, and on several occasions I have made it the basis of talks for a day's retreat.

As a child reading it I think I probably subconsciously identified in some respects with Mole. People often used to say "as blind as a mole" or "as stupid as a mole". The mole is an extraordinary little animal, hungry and thirsty, tunnelling out his strange little hill near the water, so that he has it all to himself. Like lots of animals Mole is immature until he meets with Ratty who opens him up to a new and more exciting world in which he learns to think first of others and to become like Ratty, hospitable to all.

With this as a background, two of us boys, Laurie and me, aged 11, enjoyed having our "den" in a 10-acre field of bracken and undergrowth which adjoined the back of Laurie's parents' house. On one memorable occasion we returned to basics and tried to light a fire from a clump of dry grass with two flints. However, this failed to work out and so we resorted to matches. The clump of grass flamed and in no time at all, to our alarm, had spread to some of the surrounding grass and gorse. No amount of beating it prevented it from spreading – it even made it worse and so we decided that the only thing to do was to run away. We tore down the lane on to the road and into Laurie's parents' house where his mother was waiting to give us tea.

We sat down, somewhat nervously at the table overlooking the back garden and at the 10-acre field, when his mother looked out of the window, exclaiming, "Oh dear, there's a fire on the field. It looks as if it is quite near our back hedge". We said nothing, and then there was the sound of fire engines and people shouting and looking to see how near the fire came to the houses. Fortunately, it finally subsided with just half of the field becoming scorched and blackened.

I do not recall whether Laurie or I owned up to our parents, but I do remember that some days later a boy from our school came up to me and terrified me by saying: "I know who lit that fire on the 10-acre field. It was you! I saw you running away from it." He then added, "Unless you give me half-a-crown" – which was a lot of money at that time – "I'll tell the police." I do not recall whether or not I complied with his demand, but I do remember how frightened I was.

Fire has, in some ways, punctuated my life. Many years later a fire severely damaged St. Joseph's Church in Aylesbury where I was parish priest. On that occasion it was started by a young lad, and psychiatrists claimed it was because he had experienced a bad day at school. Then, as I write, there are the bush fires in Australia. And also, recently, there was the much publicised fire in Notre Dame Cathedral, Paris, where I have been ordained. Long prior to this, also in France, there was the fire of battle in World War I when the British soldiers were advancing on Amiens in August 1918, and my father was wounded by flying shrapnel in his right arm.

It is worth recounting how immediately following this injury my father was shipped back to England to a hospital in Lincolnshire. Enroute the train carrying the injured passed through Acton where my father's parents lived. When my father realised this, he asked someone on the train to fill in one of the official postcards, addressing it to his parents, and had it thrown out of the carriage window as it passed through Acton station. The postcard was picked up by someone, posted to his parents, and this was the first news they had of their son being wounded and back in England. This of course was long before the days of mobile phones.

After lengthy treatment in hospital and losing the use of his right hand, he had to learn to write with his left hand and play the piano using only one finger of his right hand. In his old age, however, he managed to type out his memoirs ("Chronicles of a Century") on my mother's old typewriter. His eyesight had also deteriorated in his early seventies when he had to stop driving but instead went out for regular walks, often with myself or a friend, Mary, Judith or Jock. After the death of my mother he became like an older brother to me. My father together with my mother, have had a tremendous influence for good in all that I have achieved, and my father's experience in WW1 caused me to read and re-read many times with emotion, Paul Gallico's book "The Snow Goose" and the escape from Dunkirk in World War II.

After this preamble what follows is an attempt at discerning the work of God in various aspects of my life. This involves, first of all, God's presence in the beauty of drama, music, sculpture and painting, in the loving acts of several remarkable people whom I have known and then, finally, his Presence in prayer, death, resurrection and the Trinity.

Chapter 2

Drama, Music, Sculpture and Painting

"The Kingdom of God is among you" (Luke 17 – 21)

"A thing of beauty is a joy forever; its loveliness increases; it will never pass into nothingness, but still will keep a bower quiet for us and a sleep. Full of sweet dreams, and health, and quiet breathing" (John Keats).

Leading people first of all to what is beautiful in the Church, in life and religion, will help them later, to discover what is good and true. God is present in all that is beautiful, and I have tried to show this in what follows.

One of my mother's great strengths was her voice. She had a diploma in elocution, and it is thanks to her guidance and encouragement that I have developed a good speaking voice and an interest in drama. Thus, it was that, whilst at Hull studying for a General Science degree in Pure Maths, Applied Maths, Logic and Scientific Methodology (quite a mouthful) much of my spare time was taken up with the Dramatic Society. Anthony Brown, who later became a professional actor, encouraged me, and when he left I took over the running of the Drama Group.

I then persuaded Dame Sybil Thorndike and Sir Lewis Casson to be vice-presidents of our group. On one occasion when they were on tour playing in the local theatre in Hull, we decided to invite them to tea to meet other members of the Dramatic Society. We sat with them in the corner of the students' common room and found them interested in all that we were doing. They, in their own turn, regaled us with some of their experiences. At one point I asked if they ever became bored by acting out the same part night after night. "Oh no," replied Dame Sybil. "You see, every audience is different. You can smell an audience" And she placed a particular emphasis on the word "smell". "Have you noticed that?" she added. We knew what she meant.

As we bade them farewell, expressing our enthusiasm at the prospect of seeing them in the play that evening, Dame Sybil sank back on the seat of the taxi we had ordered for them (students didn't have cars in those days), laughed and thanking us, said, "Well, I hope we can smell you tonight!" Lewis and Sybil's son John Casson, wrote a fascinating biography of his parents.

In my final year at University College, Hull, I developed an interest in the writings of G.K. Chesterton. Reading some of his books, especially "Orthodoxy", led me to finding out more about the Catholic faith. This also led to the discovery of a play written by Chesterton and which had not been performed in any theatre in England. It was called the "The Surprise" and it concerns a Franciscan Friar who, while wandering among the foothills of the Pyrenees in the sixteen century encounters a master puppet-maker (known as the Author) who owns a complete set of puppets who act and talk just like human beings in plays written for them by the Author. The Friar is interested in the puppets and the Author agrees to let him see one of the plays. It turns out to be a delightfully poetic little fairy-tale drama in which, as the Author points out to the Friar when it is all over, there is not one evil deed. All the puppets behave themselves perfectly, and the play reaches a perfect, happy-ever-after conclusion. So like human beings are these puppets that the Author wishes they had minds and wills of their own. At the culmination of a big semi-philosophical dialogue between the Author and the Friar, the latter works a miracle and the puppets march on to the stage as real human beings possessing free will. Then, while the Friar looks on and the Author retires in amazement to the steps of the caravan, the puppets re-enact their play; but this time there is a difference, for with free will things do not turn out as before. In fact, the original play is completely spoilt and two of the characters start fighting. The Author is by this time so disturbed by the way in which the play has been ruined that he calls out to them: "What do you think you are doing with my play? Drop it! Stop! I am coming down." And on this note the play ends.

The religious symbolism of the whole play is, on the surface, fairly obvious: the creation by God of man, in the first place perfect, and then, through freewill, his fall. The puppet play itself is permeated by Chesterton's philosophy of surprise: "Blessed is he that expecteth nothing for he shall be gloriously surprised". But the final surprise, the intervention by the Author, is of course the greatest of all, and leaves the audience with a big question mark.

Towards the end of 1960 when the prayers of the Mass were beginning to be said in the vernacular, there was also a relaxation generally of the rituals involved. This allowed for the music of the celebration to include other instruments than the organ. I felt that this was the means of enabling the liturgy to become a real celebration and so whilst I was chaplain at the RAF Cosford, near Wolverhampton, I, with the help of Mel Smith, a civilian helper, formed a small guitar group to accompany the hymns.

Soon after this, when I left the RAF, I invited the group, the Acorns, one Sunday to visit my new parish of SS Philip and James in Bedford. This was the beginning of another group being formed and soon after in the early 1970s we invited Kevin Mayhew and Joan McCrimmon to organise a Folk Music Day at nearby Clapham Park Convent. One of our parishioners Marie Rock persuaded her non-Catholic husband Gordon to attend.

In the course of the day there was a workshop at which the participants were invited to set to music a part of the Mass. Gordon who was head of music at the Pilgrim School in Bedford chose the Gloria. Kevin Mayhew was impressed by this and suggested that Gordon should set the whole of the Mass to music. Within a few days scribbling odd phrases of music in a notebook as he drove to school, the complete Mass took shape. Gordon referred to me regarding a few details and finally sent it off to Kevin who agreed to publish it as the Pilgrim Mass and insisted on dedicating it to me. This was the first of several Masses written by Gordon and they became popular in many English-speaking countries.

During this time Gordon decided that he ought to "join the club" and I had the great pleasure of receiving him into the Catholic Church. He was full of energy and ideas and for thirteen years, until he retired, was the Headmaster of Duston Upper School, near Northampton. This was a very busy and somewhat pressurised role and he once told me that, in order to cope he would quite often, at lunchtime, put an "engaged" notice on the outside of his office door, and for twenty minutes lie flat on the floor, breathing steadily and relaxing. He always had great energy and an enthusiastic love of life which overflowed into his numerous compositions.

In Twelfth Night a character claims that "if music be the food of love, play on; give me excess of it". This is how I feel about Mozart's music that I could listen to all day. His music is so full of life and energy and this is the more surprising, considering his difficult childhood and unhappy marriage. He was often seen smiling, laughing and exuding a great sense of joy which is so evident in his music.

He was born in 1756 in Salzburg, an Austrian city that he came to dislike. At an amazingly early age he played the clavichord. He was encouraged and one might say pushed into performing concerts by his father Leopold, who had an eye on financial rewards. By the age of six, Leopold arranged for the whole family to make an European tour involving concerts in London which was the cultural centre at the time. It was there that he composed several of his first symphonies. When they finally returned to Salzburg, Leopold regretfully accepted the fact that, due to ill health he would have to allow his now seventeen and half year old son to continue his travels with his mother.

Thus it was that Wolfgang and his mother went first to Augsburg, their home town and stayed for a while near other members of their family. These included several attractive female cousins, with one of whom Wolfgang developed a close relationship. The later correspondence between them is punctuated with a great deal of toilet humour, of which Wolfgang was a past master. None of this, however seems to have prevented him from writing several symphonies and many other shorter works.

Wolfgang and his mother journeyed on to Paris where his mother became ill and died. The relationship between Wolfgang and his father, who had stayed in Salzburg was increasingly strained and Wolfgang finally settled in Vienna, married one of the daughters of the family he was staying with, became comfortably off and had two sons, the second one who was born shortly before Wolfgang fell into serious debt due to his extravagances and living beyond his means. He was always high-spirited and in the few years towards the end of his life he composed several operas, the very popular clarinet concerto, the Ave Verum Corpus and most of the Requiem which he was still composing when he lay on his bed and died on 5th December 1791.

Michael Royde-Smith, the nephew of the novelist, suffered in his earlier years from schizophrenia. This caused him to be a patient in St Andrew's Hospital, Northampton. However, Michael was a skilled sculptor and was responsible for the statue of St Gregory on the exterior façade of the Catholic Church of that name in Northampton. I knew Michael quite well when I was a curate at St Gregory's in the early 1960s and on one occasion, in the course of conversation, I happened to mention that I had yet to see a representation or statue of the Sacred Heart that wasn't sloppy and slushy. Michael must have taken my remark on board, for some ten months later he suddenly announced to me: "Father, I have just finished your Sacred Heart!" He then uncovered a slab of stone which he had extracted from a corner of a local cemetery, beautifully carved with the quotation from Ezekiel, "I will take away the stony heart from their midst and give them a heart of flesh". This merged into the outline shape of the heart.

Michael's own description of this masterpiece is worth quoting:

> *EZEKIEL XI 19*
> *"This work affirms The Presence of Christ in the human heart.*
> *From a stone tablet a heart-shaped portion is removed and in*
> *the recess so made the crucified form, amidst attendant wings*
> *is carved as if emerging into consciousness. The legend is a*
> *variant of Ezekiel XI 19 which reference is used as a*
> *provisional title. (The word midst, where the Vulgate has*
> *"carne", was put instead of "flesh" in a belief not untinged*
> *with concern for euphony that it occurred in a valid English*
> *version of this text.)"*

The initial letter "I" may by reason of its relatively bold cutting, suggest a blow dealt to humanity, the italics following, cut around the recess, veins or thickening heat.
The use of capitals for the latter part of the text cut within the recess, is proclamatory.
It was from the idea of using lettering to indicate wounds that the design grew. Not infelicitously the letter "A" was available to indicate the wound in the heart of Jesus – "I am alpha" he said "in the beginning, who also speak unto you". The compression and unevenness, not to say derangement of this part of the inscription, may be found eloquent of the turmoil of the human heart.

The Sacred Heart by Michael Royde-Smith was begun in October 1963. It was included in the Northampton Town and County Art Society's Golden Jubilee Exhibition at the Art Gallery, Guildhall Road, Northampton, and the same year acquired by me. The material of which it is made is a strong and durable limestone probably from a quarry in the neighbourhood of Northampton not now used.

"The Goldfinch" is a novel by the American author, Donna Tartt. It has recently been made into a film, and it is a story of a young lad Theo whose parents are divorced. He has been in some sort of trouble at school and he is on his way with his mother to see the headmaster.

They arrived at the school early and so his mother suggests they visit the museum of art which his mother is always keen on going to. After looking at various works of art his mother shows him her favourite painting which is a fairly small one of a bird, a goldfinch, chained to a perch. She talks to Theo about it and then, as there is still time, she leaves Theo and goes to visit the gift shop.

Suddenly there is a terrible explosion, a terrorist attack, and many are killed including Theo's mother. Theo himself is covered with rubble but reaches out and clings to the goldfinch painting just near him. He managed to leave the art gallery, still clutching the painting and he keeps it hidden away as it is so precious to him reminding him of his mother.

The police are looking for the painting but he keeps it carefully hidden, until one day he goes to see his father and befriends a boy who drinks and is on drugs, and in a foolish moment he shows the painting to his friend, who secretly takes the painting and wraps up the parcel again so that Theo does not realise what has happened. Many years later whilst Theo, still thinks he has the painting, his friend owns up to what he has done, but by this time the painting has been sold and used for bad purposes.

Bishop Robert Barron in his "Word on Fire" video poses the question: "What do we do with precious things and people in our lives? Do we hide them away, cling to them, but then like Theo, discover that we've lost them? On the contrary we should see them and treasure them, but not hang on to them. The beautiful things and people are there to be savoured and appreciated, and then given away to others". I think of this when I look at the imaginative and inspiring painting of Chartres Cathedral, painted and given to me by the artist John Danford.

Chapter 3

Fulfilling Needs, Both Near and Far

"Come you whom my Father has blessed, take for your heritage the kingdom prepared for you since the foundation of the world. For I was hungry and you gave me food ; I was thirsty and you gave me drink; I was a stranger and you made me welcome; naked and you clothed me, sick and you visited me, in prison and you came to see me." Then the virtuous will say to him in reply, "Lord, when did we see you hungry and feed you; or thirsty and give you drink? When did we see you a stranger and make you welcome; naked and clothe you; sick or in prison and go to see you? And the King will answer, "I tell you solemnly. In so far as you did this to one of the least of these brothers of mine, you did it to me." (Mtt 2 34-37)

The theme of poverty in different forms has permeated my life and I have been inspired by those who have given their whole lives helping others in need. What follows is a taste of some of these encounters

I was introduced to Richard Carr-Gomm whilst I was parish priest in Aylesbury. It happened in this way. Frequently "men of the road" would call at the door asking for money, food or somewhere to sleep. There was a fairly small garden-cum-yard behind the church and house, in one corner of which was a small shed. One day, to meet the needs of a caller, I put a makeshift bed in this hut, but it soon turned out to be inadequate, and resulted soon in the need of a larger hut, sometimes three beds. One of the parishioners heard that I was trying to help homeless people and told me that a certain Richard Carr-Gomm had an organization to help single lonely people.

16

A meeting was arranged and I found him to be a charismatic figure who during World War II was an officer in the Grenadier Guards and continued in his regiment in peacetime. He then finally came to retirement, was asked to go with the Kabaka of Buganda to accompany him on his return from exile. However, he declined this as he had increasingly felt a need to help people who were lonely. He then did an extraordinary thing: he applied as home help in Bermondsey and spent his time visiting lonely people, scrubbing floors, doing housework, cooking and all the other menial jobs as a home help is called upon to do. It was this great desire to work among people in need – the old, the handicapped, but especially the lonely – that led him to do this, and as a result of that, shortly afterwards in 1956 to form the Abbeyfield Society together with some friends, who catered in a homely situation for elderly, lonely people. The name Abbeyfield came from the road in which Richard was living at the time. Six years later, after many such houses had been opened all over the country, there were divisions in the leadership between those who wanted to concentrate more on the material and the practical, and those who felt that the human and emotional and the spiritual were, if anything, more important. As a result of Richard Carr-Gomm opting for the latter attitude, he was dismissed from the Abbeyfield Committee by a vote of eighteen to seventeen – he, who founded it, was rejected from it! He then turned his attention to Africa and spent some time there, whilst still maintaining his ideal to help the lonely.

At the end of 1964 he was back in London and started up what came to be known as the Carr-Gomm Society. It was decided to adopt his name for the Society, as various other titles were found to be either in use already, or for various reasons undesirable. The new Carr-Gomm Society was not limited to the elderly but extended to the lonely of all ages, who came to live in houses with a housekeeper in charge of each. Since then, in the last twenty years, Carr-Gomm houses have spread throughout the country. Richard Carr-Gomm himself was reconciled with the Abbeyfield Society, and subsequently also set up the Morpeth Society, which is primarily for lonely gentlefolk and centred in London.

17

The Carr-Gomm house in Aylesbury, which I was instrumental in starting – in spite of a certain amount of opposition by people who did not think there was a need in Aylesbury for such a house – was situated not far from the High Street, on the Tring Road. It was an eight-bedroomed house, with a small flat for Jane Boothroyd who was appointed the first housekeeper. Within a few weeks we had filled it. Some mistakes were at first made in the allocation of rooms, but we learned through experience. It was an old house in a very bad state of repair, which had to be renovated and some of the rooms divided up. We had it pleasantly decorated and furnished, as we felt that a new clean and tidy atmosphere would help raise the general tone of the residents.

This was a happier arrangement than the shed in the backyard, and through it I came to know Richard Carr-Gomm quite well. We shared similar ideas, especially in the way that Richard felt that a time for prayer should be included in the daily running of the house

During my time as parish priest in St Joseph's, Aylesbury, I was introduced to Peter Benenson, who lived in a nearby village. Peter was the founder of Amnesty International, and I invited him on a Sunday to speak to our congregation about Amnesty. This he was pleased to do and began by recounting how it had all begun.

Peter read in a newspaper article about two Portuguese students who had been arrested and sentenced to seven years imprisonment. They had been in a restaurant drinking a toast to freedom at a time when Salazar was in power. This so enraged Peter when he read about it as he was travelling on a London bus, and his first inclination was to go to the Portuguese embassy to protest, but then on second thoughts he got off the bus and went into the Church of St Martin in the Fields and prayed there. As a result of this he wrote to David Aster who was the editor of the Observer and David put an article in the paper. "The forgotten prisoners". He asked readers to write letters showing their support for the students. Very soon to coordinate this letter writing campaign, Amnesty International was founded in 1961 by Benenson and six others. The response was overwhelming and groups of letter writers were formed in many other countries.

On one of many trips to France I took with me a group from Bedford, and in the course of visiting some of the sights of Paris we called at the Siloe Bar Restaurant in the Boulevard Clichy. This important venture in the centre of Paris and beneath the shadow of the Sacre' Coeur Basilica, began nearly twenty years earlier in 1965 when a young man of 25 spent his time recruiting suitable girls for strip-tease turns, and prostitution. He began to see the error of his ways, met a local priest and lived for a time in a local presbytery where he talked about his former "work". The problem in this part of Paris – as elsewhere – was that the organised Church had hardly any contact with the prostitutes, drug addicts, tramps, transvestites etc. The Parish Priest and his Assistant felt that something should be done – but what?

A non-profit Association, founded by Paul Claudel and called the Association Siloe was formed, and included a group of women who made friends with some of the prostitutes. They reflected a great deal on the problem; and about this time an old man who had been running a Bar Restaurant in the Bld. Clichy gave it up, and with the help of a gift from the Papal Nuncio and the support of the Archbishop, the restaurant was purchased – and then run as a profit-making venture, separate from the Association Siloe. A priest was present and instrumental in the running of the Bar-Restaurant, together with helpers, not all of whom were Christians. The Bar-Restaurant and its running is completely accepted in the neighbourhood and is well frequented by the above mentioned people, who are in general, rejected by society.

Two hostels have also been opened – one for men and the other for women – to accommodate those who may be ready to take a return step towards normal life. The priest in the Bar-Restaurant is involved

for them by the Author. The Friar is interested in the puppets and th
Author agrees to let him see one of the plays. It turns out to be a
delightfully poetic little fairy-tale drama in which, as the Author poin
out to the Friar when it is all over, there is not one evil deed. All the
puppets behave themselves perfectly, and the play reaches a perfect,
happy-ever-after conclusion. So like human beings are these puppets
that the Author wishes they had minds and wills of their own. At the
culmination of a big semi-philosophical dialogue between the Author
and the Friar, the latter works a miracle and the puppets march on to
the stage as real human beings possessing free will. Then, while the
Friar looks on and the Author retires in amazement to the steps of the
caravan, the puppets re-enact their play; but this time there is a
difference, for with free will things do not turn out as before. In fact,
the original play is completely spoilt and two of the characters start
fighting. The Author is by this time so disturbed by the way in which

with the ministry of listening
that God loves them as and v
to see little result; however, there signs in some ⌐. ⌐ ⌐
Jesus Christ and to the Church. The work of the Bar-Restaurant and ᴉ⌐ₛ
helpers is fully recognised by the local authorities and supported by
them as an important aspect of social service work.

10

Above the Restaurant is a tiny office and even smaller areas curtained
off where there is daily Mass and where the Blessed Sacrament is
exposed continuously. When asked what particular aspect of the
project we could perhaps pray for, Father – with some diffidence –
said he needed the support of prayer for strength and courage to be
able to respond to the needs of the situation and for his faith to be
confirmed, despite the fact of not seeing results from his work. He
asked for prayers for the prostitutes that they might see God's love
and have hope – and finally, to be able to recognise Jesus Christ in
everyone frequenting the Bar-Restaurant.

I was welcomed on five occasions in Jamaica (1994, 1999, 2000, 2001,
2002) and once in 2004 in the Philippines. My first visit to Jamaica set
the tone for subsequent visits, all of which were marked by such a
genuinely warm and joyful welcome by the Missionaries of the Poor
and by Father Richard Ho Lung, in particular, who has been responsible
for feeding, housing and caring for many thousands of otherwise
homeless and abandoned people of all ages in different parts of the
world. It is an amazing story of a man, Father Richard Ho Lung, with a
vision, acted out with enthusiasm and trust in God's guidance. He has
been rightly described as humble, charismatic, a man of deep faith and
of vision, with a great sense of humour that is playful and committed.

My friendship with Richard began in 1972 whilst I was priest in the
parish on the edge of Bedford in England. One day a parishioner,
Loretta Williams, told me that her brother a Jesuit priest was coming
from Jamaica where he was teaching, to spend a few weeks' holidays

is, when I left the RAF, I invited the group, the Acorns,
o visit my new parish of SS Philip and James in Bedford.
beginning of another group being formed and soon after
1970s we invited Kevin Mayhew and Joan McCrimmon to
olk Music Day at nearby Clapham Park Convent. One of
oners Marie Rock persuaded her non-Catholic husband
attend.

rse of the day there was a workshop at which the
ts were invited to set to music a part of the Mass. Gordon
head of music at the Pilgrim School in Bedford chose the
Kevin Mayhew was
should set the who
g odd phrases of r

with her and her family. "Could he", she asked "join me in celebrating the Sunday Mass?" "Of course, delighted," I replied.

That Sunday morning I was confronted with a fairly tall, long-haired person with Chinese features in his early thirties, a smiling face, dressed casually and not, as was then the custom a Roman collar. He was carrying a large bunch of varied and coloured flowers. He smiled broadly and I welcomed him and I commented on the attractive flowers he was holding. "Yes, I thought we could decorate the altar," he responded. "Thank you", I said, "But where did you get them?" It being Sunday morning and the local shops in the respectable open-planned housing estate being closed: "Oh, I picked them from the gardens as I walked along!" he replied, still smiling.

A week or two later I had discovered that Richard had considerable musical talent, having composed many religious songs, I persuaded to him to teach our enthusiastic music group, and later, the congregation, some of his lovely compositions. It was easy launching them on everyone, as at that time, we used an overhead projector, enabling words and music to be learned and followed by all.

Richard came again the following year, but then several years elapsed before we caught up with each other and during this time he had left the Jesuit order and told me, enthusiastically, that he was now working with the poor and homeless in Jamaica. "Come and see what we're doing," he invited me. "You could stay in the Cathedral house up the road or with the Brothers where we live." I agreed to go, and in a rash moment I opted to stay with the Brothers. This turned out to be in a dormitory fitted with bunk beds, mosquito nets and an abundance of small mosquitoes which had mastered the technique of penetrating most of the nets. Arriving after dark and out of consideration for those already asleep, negotiating the bed, the mosquito net, the single sheet and unpacking the essentials for the night, was quite a hazardous experience, following as it did the introduction to some of the Brothers who had waited up for me; it was a challenge trying to remember all their names. Far more challenging was the introduction the following day to the homeless and destitute that Richard was caring for. It is not easy to encapsulate the enthusiastic spirit, the vision, the compassion and the humour and talents of a man who has responded so completely to the will of God and all that this has meant for him and indeed for all of us.

On one occasion when I stayed with the brothers in Naga City in the Philippines I visited the nearby State-run mental hospital. This was one of the most horrifying experiences of my life. There were two main single-storey buildings, one for men, and the other for women. A veranda ran alongside the men's section and off this there were four large rooms with concrete floors (they were formerly earthen). Along one side about four feet from the ground there were closely barred openings letting in a little light and air. The doors were heavily barred and padlocked. As I approached, naked arms and hands pushed through spaces between the bars to shake my hand and faces appeared clustering for recognition.

I found a gap to look between the heads that seemed to block nearly every opening. Inside the largest of the rooms, about 40 ft by 30 ft, there was no furniture, no beds, cupboards, nothing except a few dirty mats on the floor or along a concrete ledge which ran along one wall. On the floor there were pools of liquid which, by the smell I identified as urine. In one corner there was a small area enclosed by a low wall, a hole in the ground and a water tap. This was the toilet and wash-place. In this, the largest of the rooms 34 men were confined.

The other rooms were smaller with fewer inmates, and the smallest had just a few men who frequently, if found to be violent, would be chained around the ankles and wrists. Many of the men were completely naked. They spent all their time in this confinement, food being passed under the bars of the door. All self-respect was absent, and animals would have been treated better. The women's section was similar, although not quite so dark and gloomy, and there were a few beds with iron springs but no mattresses. Some of the women were also naked.

The Brothers who took me there advised me not to write to the authorities as this would inevitably lead to them not being allowed to visit. This was the only bright spot in the lives of these poor people.

On a brighter note, the Jamaican Missionaries of the Poor Ecumenical Music Group came for ten days in June 1994. Fifteen of them had to be met on 7 different flights, 2 different airports and spread over 4 days. Several of us were involved in meeting and welcoming them. We took them to Cambridge and Walsingham where they took part in the Caribbean pilgrimage with about 1,000 people present and Northampton Cathedral was nearly full with 700 people enjoying the lively music, dancing and singing in typical West Indian style.

To continue our support of the work of the Missionaries of the Poor we now have a support group which is a recognised charity and all the donations received go directly to supply the needs of the homeless and destitute in a number of countries including Jamaica, India, the Philippines, Indonesia, Kenya and Uganda. None of the money donated goes on administration.

Katey Dougan, a Saint Louis sister, spent a number of years helping the poor and needy and by her life spreading the Good News of the Kingdom in Brazil. Prior to this she was involved in parish work in Aylesbury where she was a great help to me.

Much of what follows finds an echo in Pope Francis' published "Exhortation" "The Joy of the Gospel", in which he was clearly influenced by his own ministry in South America, and by liberation theology. He has close ties with the Church's social practices and in particular its concern for the poor. Similar problems have since occurred in Europe: the problem of keeping the Christian faith and practice alive in the absence of clergy. Pope Francis has said that we must have "a poor church for the poor". I have taken the liberty of developing this theme much as it occurs in Clodovis Boff's book. "Feet on the Ground Theology".

The church in Brazil, and especially in the country areas, is one where you really feel the Spirit of Christ, where there is Christian joy and fellowship and love amongst its members. To be a pastoral worker, sister or a priest requires great courage and determination, as the conditions, especially in the jungle and poorer areas, are very hard. There are countless examples of the church functioning in its mission for the poor but only in certain areas is it the church of the poor, and very rarely a poor church. Clodovis Boff in his book writes:

> "The whole point is to see if this "for the poor" is heading towards becoming "with the poor" so that it will eventually become an "of the poor". This is a historical process that advances by a twofold movement, the church coming closer to the poor and becoming identified with them and the poor emerging within the church as ecclesial agents. This is the option for the poor and for the poor as leaders – at first potentially and then in reality. "Church of the poor" is both an ideal and an emerging process". However, on a more optimistic note it is very often the poor who are giving evidence of the presence of the Kingdom of God here and now. There are times when the poor are embarrassed by their poverty, but in fact the opposite should be true: we should be embarrassed by our relative prosperity. Boff later continues "One young man had been waiting in the endless line at the gas station from 4 am until 3 pm. Eleven hours in line. Only then he could get a gallon of diesel fuel and that was what we were using. He didn't make a fuss about his long wait. He scarcely mentioned it. And others weren't surprised. But I was very impressed: waiting a whole day for a gallon of fuel. "You didn't eat?" I asked him. "No – otherwise I'd lose my place in line". He didn't talk like someone who thought he'd been wronged. No question about it, what the ordinary people

*have to suffer goes unheard. They don't have anyone to
complain to, unlike the upper classes who, at the least
inconvenience, have the public media to blare out their
complaints. Poverty and suffering go together like twins. And
the poor suffer not only from the nonsatisfaction of biological
needs, but also from moral injustices, humiliation, pressure,
oppression, persecution."*

We are reminded of the life of Jesus. He was born poor, lived poorly,
possessed nothing and died as one rejected by his own people. He
enjoyed no privileges or titles and often had nowhere to lay his head.
However, it is true to say that, for us, being poor, we become less
frenzied and preoccupied with the trivia of life. Do we in fact find the
poor happier and more joyful: the joy of the Gospel?

The shortage of priests is paramount throughout Brazil and in
consequence training courses are most important for lay leaders.
Sometimes these pose a problem as it is not always possible for them
to attend. Excuses are sometimes made: distance to go and work with
the rubber. However, when these difficulties are overcome there is
great enthusiasm. Often a priest is involved, not as a leader, but just
by being present, giving guidance when necessary. Lay leaders, when
properly trained become the pillars of a community. The training
often involves looking in detail at the life of the early church as
recounted in the Acts of the Apostles. This involves fidelity to the
word of God, a community of possessions, the breaking of bread,
prayer, and above all, joy.

In Greece it is said that there are just three things to do: eat, sleep,
and talk. In Australia, which I come to next, the talking centres
invariably on one of three topics: sport, nature and food! Australia has
always held an attraction for me, as one of my earliest memories was
during WWII my grandparents received regular food parcels from a
cousin who lived in Brisbane. I recall the thrill of opening the parcels

which contained tins of meat, fruit cake and other items which were unattainable in war stricken England.

Many years later when I was Dean in Northampton Cathedral I had a request from Bankstown City choir in Sydney, New South Wales who wanted to put on a concert in our Cathedral, it being the first stop in their tour of England. There were fifty-nine of them from all walks of life, nationalities, professions and all age groups with one common interest, that of love of choral music and its performance. I arranged accommodation for them all in the homes of various parishioners, giving them a taste of English home life. For the concert they were all dressed in pale green costumes and sang some classical, some church music and some typical Australian songs to a packed Cathedral.

On the morning following the concert I took them all to the cemetery in Northampton where Caroline Chisholm is buried. They needed no reminder as to who she was, as, born and buried in Northampton she became a great social reformer in Australia in the mid-nineteenth century with her head appearing on the Australian five dollar note. We all stood around her grave early on a fine summer morning and spontaneously burst into singing an appropriate song reminding ourselves of many events in the life of this amazing woman.
Caroline was actually born outside Northampton. Her father was a farmer and she was the youngest of several children. It was an open and hospitable household and Caroline herself recounts how, on one occasion when she was a young girl, her parents saw a stranger in the street and some local lads were shouting and throwing sticks at him. It turned out that he was from France and was a Roman Catholic priest forced to flee from France at the time of the Revolution. Caroline's family took him in and looked after him for some time, until he was able to journey on to stay with one of the English Catholic families who had retained their Catholic faith. The event had a profound influence on Caroline and when, a few years later, she fell in love with one of the young officers from the nearby barracks, a Lt. Archibald Chisholm, who was a Catholic, any reservations she may have had vanished. They

were married in December 1830. This was a courageous act on her part.

Archibald was posted to India and Caroline followed him soon after. She then had the difficult task of accustoming herself to a very different way of life, for she soon set up the world's first crèche in Madras. The conditions of the wives and daughters of the soldiers there were dreadful, involved in crime and prostitution. Caroline immediately set up a school for them. Her action was well ahead of her time and continued for several years until Archibald began to suffer from ill-health and was advised to take two years secondment. After much discussion Archibald and Caroline together with their two children and three Indian servants decided to venture on the long journey to Australia.

At that time Australia was known as little more than a place for banished criminals, strange wild animals and scorching heat. The Chisholms settled first of all in Sydney but it was not long before Caroline was horrified by the sight of women in a similar condition to those she had helped in Madras. There were girls from England and Ireland who were seeking a better life, but in order to survive, were caught up in prostitution and crime.

Caroline decided to do something to help them. She got the Government to give her a former immigration hostel where the girls were able to live and an employment office to help them find suitable work and, not infrequently, suitable husbands. The journey by ship from England to Australia was perilous and when Caroline returned to England in the mid-1840s she was instrumental in improving the conditions on the ships and often arranged for free passage for the girls. Throughout Australia she set up hospitals and schools for the girls and soon became well-known as the Immigrants' Friend.

When, finally, she returned to England, exhausted and ill, all of her and Archibald's resources having been spent on helping others, she died on

25th March 1870 in poverty and obscurity. Her grave, together with that of her husband, is well kept, but hardly noticeable in Billing Road Cemetery, Northampton, and it should be recognised as that of a very great Englishwoman.

So it was that when, a few years after the visit of the Australian choir, I had the opportunity to visit my relatives in Brisbane, I was able to speak knowledgeably about Caroline Chisholm and to appreciate something of the situation, though since changed, of life in Australia. Skyscrapers are now in the centre of Brisbane surrounded by thousands of individually designed single-storied Queenslander dwellings with iron roofs and built on stumps, the lower area often bricked in to provide extra storage or garage space. The nights are often disturbed by the sound of koalas playing on the roof. A fashionable touristic custom is to cuddle a koala bear, but this I refrained from doing as they invariably wee all over you.

Three further "Encounters" are worth mentioning:

An outreach for children is provided by "Mary's Meals". This is described on the cover of the book, "The Shed That Fed a Million Children" written by the founder Magnus Macfarlane-Barrow and his aim is for every child to be able to receive at least one good meal every day. This is entirely possible in this world of plenty, a world in which £12.20 can feed a child for a whole year. This is yet another book well worth reading and a cause to support.

Dunc Dyason MBE, escaped from an early life of crime and came near to suicide, but was unexpectedly converted to Christianity through hearing God's voice calling him, and he finally became involved in youth work in the local Anglican Church in Chesham Bois, near Amersham. Then, one evening he saw a BBC documentary entitled "They shoot children, don't they?" and this inspired him in 1991 to move to Guatemala. I just got home on Sunday, turned on the television and this programme was on," says Dunc. The documentary highlighted the plight of children, many thrown out or abandoned by their parents who were forced to live on the streets. Those youngsters, forced into a life of crime, were often shot at or beaten up by the police who should have been working to protect them. "I just knew this was something God wanted me to do, so I went to work for Toybox helping those children on the streets of Guatemala. When Toybox moved on to do other things in 2001 I founded Street Kids Direct."

He says 100 per cent of money donated to Street Kids Direct is used to help poverty-stricken Guatemala children. Many of them live in grave danger, fearing for their lives. When the Everyman documentary was made, there were 5,000 children on the streets. Now that figure has been reduced to zero according to a recent survey, but many children are still extremely vulnerable.

Recently Dunc rescued a family of six at risk of living on the streets and Street Kids works hard to prevent others going down the same route. Dunc met one boy Danny who has been selling drugs for five years. "He had committed armed robbery and was getting into more and more trouble. Three attempts had been made on his life and he is just nine-years-old," says Dunc. "He's now in a secure children's home and has started school and he's doing well. We help them get off the streets and offer them a mentoring programme in a centre they can visit every day." Dunc organises a local radio programme at Christmas-time with local people and especially children taking part.

A somewhat similar conversion story is that of Simon Reeve, whose travel programmes on BBC 2 have made a great hit. His autobiography "Step by Step" is worth reading and in the different places he visits he highlights both the good and the bad; he takes chances, ask questions, does things that are exciting, eats strange foreign food, and dives into the culture of the world, embracing risks. Throughout his travels he shows a great concern for the poor and those who are struggling.

It is appropriate to conclude this chapter with the following story, of a woman who has been used to every luxury and to great respect. She died, and when she arrived in heaven, an angel was sent to conduct her to her house. They passed many a lovely mansion and the woman thought that each one, as they come to it, must be the one allotted to her. When they had passed through the main streets they came to the outskirts, where the houses were much smaller; and on the very fringe they came to a house that was little more than a hut. "That is your house," said the conducting angel. "What, that?" said the woman, "I cannot live in that." "I am sorry," said the angel, "but that is all we could build for you with the materials you sent up."

Chapter 4

The Call: Priesthood and Marriage

"Launch out into the deep" (Luke 5 v4)

Adolescence is a time for searching and often of making mistakes. The call to write came from an outside source and was not pursued until many years later. It happened in this way. In my mid-teens I picked up a book my mother was reading. It was a novel by a prolific lady who wrote under two pseudonyms: Oliver Sandys and Countess Barcynska. She was described in the 1940s as "England's best-loved novelist". I enjoyed her novels and I was particularly interested in her autobiography "Full and Frank", in which she describes her second husband, throughout as "the man". I was intrigued by this mysterious and unnamed person and decided to write to her to enquire who he was. To my amazement at the time – she replied in her own handwriting:

> *"Your charming letter has given me the same kind of pleasure as a handful of freshly hand-picked wild flowers. Thank you for writing to me.*
> *Go on with your studies, for the way to literature is hardy and stony, but do not abandon the idea of writing. Study the short story. Study the great short story writers – Guy de Maupassant.*
> *I am quite sure, after reading your letter, that you will do something in the world of books, so keep sight of your star. You ask for the name of "the man". He was the greatest modern exponent of the short story – Caradoc Evans. He died a year ago – and that is the end of my story. I have written a biography concerning him – Caradoc Evans by Oliver Sandys – and when it is out you will be able to find out all about the life of a genius."*

And a year later she wrote:

> "I am so glad you liked the biography and the last book. If my
> writing helps you in any way in the future to become a writer
> with a view or a message then it will be alone worthwhile that
> I ever took up a pen.
> What are you destined for as regards a career?
> You have, I think, an extraordinary maturity of thought and
> expression. How few people of your age think at all?
> You know, Kenneth, I am quite certain you are going to do
> something really worthwhile and, if you keep this letter from
> fifteen to twenty years, it might prove interesting reading.
> And now about religion – you say you feel you will have to
> make a choice.
> I myself should not be surprised if you became a RC. It is a
> religion which still produces saints and has much mercy for
> sinners. I have met two saints in my own time. I feel that in
> countless ways it sustains where other religions fail.
> Chesterton's acceptance of it proves that. His great mind
> could not have followed anything claptrap or trivial."

This was the beginning of an exchange of letters, which continued until
shortly before her death in 1964. During that time, whilst on many
cycling holidays, I visited Caradoc Evan's grave at New Cross in South
Wales. The inscription on the tombstone read: "Bury me lightly so that
the soft rain may reach my face and the fluttering of the butterfly may
not escape my ear." The following year I cycled again to Wales and
decided to visit my novelist penfriend who lived near Aberystwyth. On
finally finding the address I was looking for, a bungalow, which went
by the name of Heddle meaning Peaceful Place, I propped my bicycle
by the hedge, but was then dismayed to find that no one was at home.
As it was already evening, I asked a lady living opposite whether Mrs
Caradoc Evans was away on holiday. To my relief, "No", she had only a
few moments ago walked up to the post office, which, even in the
smallest of villages, used to keep open until 7 p.m. I was also told that
Nickie, her son, was there in the adjacent field. Filled anew with a

flood of shyness, I crossed over to the field indicated and saw a man with a gun approaching. As we came within speaking distance I was just about to introduce myself when he said, heartily shaking hands, "Kenneth, Kenneth er Payne!" For the moment I was taken aback that he should seem to know me. I discovered later that it was from my photograph, which some time previously I had sent to his mother.

We walked up to the post office where I met his mother, an attractive and colourful lady in her fifties. They both wanted to know more about this strange young man who read the novels, had made a pilgrimage to meet them, was interested in religion, and who had begun finding out about the Catholic faith. They invited me to supper the following evening when we talked a lot about Catholicism – Nick had recently become a Catholic. The friendship with Mrs Caradoc Evans, sustained by occasional letters and visits- she moved later to Church Stretton in Shropshire – had a lasting effect on me, and taught me the importance and influence that an older person outside the family can have on a younger person, through their welcome, their interest and their encouragement.

Reading a number of books about religion. Christianity and Catholicism in particular, led me one day in 1948 to ask Suzanne Ackermann, the French wife of a colleague of my father, if I could accompany her to a Sunday Mass. She was delighted but not so pleased when the sermon turned out to be about the evils of divorce. However, I was quite struck by the authoritative way in which the priest explained the Church's teaching.

Some months later I went on my own to the little Catholic Church of St. Edward the Confessor, situated in Sutton Park near where we lived. Father Gordon Albion was the parish priest and after the Mass I very nervously knocked on the door of the sacristy and stammered out, "I think I want to become a Catholic". Father Albion was a well-known historian and broadcaster and clearly a busy man, but immediately replied. "All right, come and see me next Wednesday at 3 pm." This became the first of just five instructions which due to holidays and other commitments was all I had before being baptised in the Catholic Church. Father guided me in my reading and encouraged me to take part in some of his broadcast services.

Throughout this time I was, as already related, very involved with the Dramatic Society, and one of the plays we put on was Sheridan's "The Rivals". This we took to Germany producing it in several German universities. I played the part of Captain Jack Absolute, and this led me to falling in love with my opposite number, Lydia Languish. Vivian, who took this part, and I became unofficially engaged to be married until I had ideas about the priesthood. This gave rise to agonising months of doubt and indecision for both of us and we finally resolved to break off our relationship. Fortunately, Vivian eventually became happily married to Trevor, whilst I pursued the call to priesthood. We occasionally exchanged letters and twice met before she died a few years ago. We had made a difficult decision, a leap in the dark for each of us.

The priest who helped me most towards the priesthood whilst I was doing my national service at Halton, near Aylesbury, was a Benedictine from Downside. After gaining a commission I reported to the senior education officer at RAF Halton, who looked at me and then looked at the file on the desk in front of him. "I see your subject is mathematics".
"Yes, Sir" I replied.
"Well," he continued, "we've enough officers already teaching mathematics, but we need more to take engineering drawing". He paused.
"What's that, Sir?" I countered quite seriously.
"Oh, it's an easy and interesting subject to teach. Flight Lieutenant Durrant is an expert. Go and talk to him and there are books in the library." Then, to my further alarm he added, "Today's Tuesday. You could start next Monday! By the way," he continued, "I see you're a RC. There's a very fine RC chaplain here, a Father Brookes. See me in the bar before lunch and I'll introduce you to him." This he duly did, and I found immediately that Father Brookes was someone who was

open and approachable. We became good friends and through him I was able to experience something of the Benedictine spirituality at Downside, meet Abbot Christopher Butler, who later became a bishop and whom I often met many years later when we were both on the editorial board of the Clergy Review.

> *Father Rudesind Brookes, a very gifted priest, was in the Irish Guards during WWI prior to becoming a monk at Downside. In his Memoirs he gives the following description of himself: "I was born in London on14th March 1898. Many of my friends think of me as a typical Englishman, but that is far from the truth. My real name is Count John Charles Hugo de Minciaky, a fact of which I remained ignorant until the age of sixteen. My father, Count Emile Maria de Minciaky, was Russian from Georgia, a Roman Catholic, and at the time of my birth an Attache' at the Imperial Russian Embassy to the Court of St James, which was in St Petersburg Square, Bayswater. My mother, Beatrix, was Swedish and a Lutheran, her father being Eric Hugo Waldenstrom, but her mother, Elizabeth Hannaway, was Irish. I am therefore half Russian, a quarter Swedish and a quarter Irish. My parents were married on 27 August 1892, by Father Frederick Antrobus at the Brompton Oratory. They were subsequently divorced and my mother married Warrick Brookes in 1900 and later bore him a daughter, my half-sister Claire, some three years after my own birth."*

Early on, during his service in the Brigade of Guards, he recounts that one of his friends, Eddie Fitz Clarence, who later became the Earl of Munster, was a very debonair young blade and it was to him that he owed his nickname "Dolly". Up to that time," he writes," I had usually been known as "Brookie", but one day Eddie gave me a scurrilous book to read called "The Adventures of Dolly Varden." I was not a prude and I certainly had no thought then of becoming a priest, but I had no time for that sort of book and I threw it down on the sofa, saying "I can't waste my time reading that rubbish", whereupon Eddie exclaimed: "Oh Dolly!" and the nickname stuck and has remained with me all my life."

Father Dolly thought, at one point, that I might be destined to join the Benedictine Community at Downside, but this was not to be, as, after much thought and prayer, it was arranged that I should offer myself to be trained for the priesthood in the Northampton Diocese. However, I took with me the Benedictine motto "Ora et labora" which I had inscribed on the base of the chalice, given to me by my parents at my ordination, and which I have used ever since. Father Brookes arranged for me to go to see Bishop Leo Parker, who at that point was staying at Thornton Convent. I travelled by car with Fr Brookes, and I recall how, throughout the journey, Father repeatedly warned me not to be put off by the Bishop. "He's a very rude man; a very rude man, but don't let that put you off." In the event I found almost the opposite to be true. He questioned me about my desire to be a priest and my motivation and ended by telling me that he would let me know to which seminary he would send me. I subsequently had a soft spot for Bishop Leo, and always grateful to him for sending me to St Sulpice in Paris for five years' study as soon as I completed my National Service in the RAF. Prior to leaving RAF Halton and beginning my studies at the seminary, Father Brookes came with me to visit my parents. The purpose of this was to try to soften the blow that their only son was embarking on a celibate vocation in the Roman Catholic priesthood. I think Father Brookes made quite a hit with my parents and eased the blow to such an extent that five years later they agreed to travel to Paris for my ordination in Notre Dame Cathedral. After five very happy, although in some ways difficult, years in Paris, I began to think about my ordination. Forty-three of us were to be ordained in Notre-Dame Cathedral. Others were ordained in their own dioceses in France and elsewhere. My parents were interested in coming over for it, as also were several other friends. The ordination was scheduled to begin at 8.30 a.m.

The Parisians all had family luncheon celebrations organised in their homes. What was I to do? I began to make enquiries for a modest restaurant with a private room available where I could gather with some fourteen or so people. Then, one Thursday whilst I was tidying up after the weekly catechism class in the local parish, Madame Jeanne Lochet, an energetic and skilled catechist in her mid-forties and whom I was understudying, came up to me and asked, "What are you going to do after your ordination – with your parents and friends?" I explained my predicament, and then, without a moment's hesitation she said, "Venez chez moi! (Come to my house) – and I will prepare the lunch for you all." In the even we all went to her cousin's flat nearby as her own in the Rue du Bac would have been too small. Jeanne had six offsprings and was widowed soon after the birth of her sixth. Her eldest son had begun training for the priesthood, another was in law and a third was destined to be a veterinary surgeon. The three daughters followed various professions, and in later years I came to know the whole family as a sort of French extension to my own. The English Channel saw many crossings to and fro, by air, by boat, and more recently by train; and all that was as a result of that spontaneous and understanding phrase, "Venez chez moi!"

Such was one of the many wonderful families whom I have had the pleasure of knowing over the years. I later became involved in the Teams of our Lady, or Equipes de Notre Dame, which helped me to appreciate, even more, the value of the Sacrament of Marriage. This movement in the Church organised in 1939, just before WWII by a young priest, Father Henri Cafferel who answered his presbytery door one evening to a young couple who asked him, "Father how can we live more fully the Sacrament of Marriage?" He talked with them and the following week they came again, with several couples, to continue the conversation.

There followed from this the idea of regular meetings of couples with a priest, the individual couples agreeing to pray alone and together each day, to read the scriptures and each month have a "sit-down" to share their joys and difficulties. After the war was over groups of couples started meeting regularly each month, and the whole idea spread rapidly to many countries. There are now well over 100,000 couples in some 60 countries who belong to the Equipes de Notre Dame.

Referring to my own experience, in November 1992, I was invited to Badby near Daventry, for a national gathering of representatives of Teams of our Lady drawn from around the country. I was asked to be a sector Chaplain. It was from this that we soon generated a number of Teams in the Northampton area. The commitment and the structure of the monthly meetings appealed to me. Little did I think then that fifteen years later I would be the Super-Regional Chaplain, covering various countries of the Trans Atlantic Super Region: South Africa, Trinidad, Malawi, Ireland, Scotland and Australia! Equipes de Notre Dame were also strong in Mauritius which I visited for the ordination of a friend.

A few years later I took part in several French Team meetings in or near Ealing. At one of these the discussion was led by a young French lady who, whilst declaiming on some quite complex issue, stood up and walked to and fro whilst breast feeding her baby!

It is not easy for a celibate priest to write about marriage in a relevant way. However, to aid me I found the books by Gary Chapman to be specifically helpful. There are, he claims, five languages of love: affirmation, quality time, receiving gifts, acts of service and physical touch. He extends these maxims to other ways of life, other vocations – single, children, adolescents and engaged couples – in fact to all conditions of people.

Contrary to the views of some, the two vocations of priesthood and marriage can co-exist in the Church, and, indeed, can result in the enrichment of all concerned. This is seen in the Orthodox churches as well as in some branches of the Catholic Church, for example, the Maronites, and we are slowly moving in that direction in the Catholic Church.

Chapter 5

Prayer: Taize and De Mello

Jesus said to his disciples: Say this when you pray:

"Our Father in heaven,
May your name be held holy,
Your kingdom come'
Your will be done,
On earth as in heaven,
Give us today our daily bread.
And forgive us our debts,
As we have forgiven those who are in debt to us.
And do not put us to the test,
But save us from the evil one."

(Mtt6 7-13)

Encounter with God in all that is beautiful, in other people and in our relationships, must, of course, include our encounter with God in prayer.

Often on a Sunday evening in the seminary a specially invited speaker would come to give a talk to us. On one occasion it was Brother Roger Schutz, the prior at Taize, the ecumenical community in the centre of France. At that time I must admit I was not particularly ecumenically minded and the Taize community was in its early stages of growth, and so I recall little of what Brother Roger shared with us. It was some years later that I took a group of young people for a week in Taize and this was the first of many visits.

Their style of worship has grown on me and I think that much of what the Taize community stands for and practises, is the way forward for the Church. On most of my regular visits to Taize at the request of the

Brothers I would be available for confessions after the evening prayer. On one such occasion, after an hour or so hearing confessions, as I left the church a lady came up to me and asked if I could go with her and her husband to where they were staying. Although, by then, it was after 10 p.m. and I was quite ready for bed, I, with some hesitation agreed as she had already spoken to me during the confessions, and probably, wanted to chat further. Cars were parked nearby, and she called out "Gus, Gus" to her husband who she thought was waiting in their car. But Gus did not appear. "Oh, he must have given up waiting for me and gone home. "Never mind" she said "we can walk".

This it turned out, was a walk in the dark unlit lane for a mile to the next village of Ameuny. As we set out it occurred to me that I was running a risk, as it was only a short time since Brother Roger had been killed by a demented lady in the church. However, all was well, and we talked about the different problems the Church has in both our countries, as it turned out that my companion was from Holland. On arriving at Ameuny, Maud, such was her name, stopped and opened the front door of one of the small cottages, again calling "Gus, Gus", who eventually came downstairs and met me. It was clear that he had given up waiting for his wife, had driven to their cottage and gone to bed. However, he rapidly adjusted himself to being hospitable, opened a bottle of wine, and we talked at length about the Church and the Taize community. Gus was a retired architect, and he and Maud lived in Ouddorp, Holland, but spent some time each year in their small cottage near Taize, enabling them to join in their daily prayer with the Brothers.

Concelebrating the Sunday Mass, as well as on week days, was always a highpoint of the week, and Brother Roger, at the end of the Mass, would always come over to speak to priests who were visitors. The following prayer exercises, devised by Fr. Anthony De Mello, link up with the approach to prayer found at Taize, and because they have been so helpful to me. I include them here. The basis of all of them is the awareness of our breathing.

(a) Exercise for Silence

Understand
Come to the realization that words and ideas are inadequate.
Meditate on this. Recall each idea you have of God and say to
yourself, "He is more unlike this than like this. He is far beyond this
and far better than this".

Look
Look at some nature scene or some object. Don't look at anything
sensational. Just look as if you are seeing it for the first time.

Listen
Listen to all the sounds around you. If possible, avoid putting names to
the sounds. Realise that each sound is really composed of many
sounds. Don't look for anything sensational. Just listen to those
sounds as if you are hearing them for the first time in your life.

Scripture
Recall your favourite sentence of Jesus from the New Testament.
Repeat it to yourself. Imagine Jesus standing in front of you and he
addresses those words to you. Don't dwell too much on the meaning
of the words. Resist the temptation to react. Don't say anything and
don't respond in any way. Let the words reverberate and resound
within you. When you cannot contain it anymore, respond to Jesus.
A variation of this exercise is to get into silence first. Then recall a
sentence from scripture or get someone to read it to you. Those
words of scripture will be etched in your heart and they will deepen
your silence. They may take on a meaning that is quite beyond the
power of words to express.

(b) Exercise for Peace

Body Awareness
Close your eyes. Get in touch with your body. Become aware of all
the sensations on the surface of your body: start at the crown of your
head and keep moving down slowly until you reach the tip of your
toes, omitting no part of the surface of your skin. Repeat the exercise
for a full half-hour or more.
If you ever get to a point where you experience sensations over the
whole surface of your body, then dwell on the awareness of your body
as a whole, teeming with sensations.

Acceptance
Say yes to everything that you find unpleasant but that you cannot
change. Say yes to whatever awaits you in the future.

Perspective
Think of some of the things you were attached to or that you feared as
a child and that no longer affect you. Think of some of the things you
are most attached to. Say to yourself a few times slowly, "This too will
pass away." Think of some of the things you dislike or fear. Say to
yourself a few times slowly, "This too will pass away."

Alternative Exercises for Busy People

Abbreviated Body Awareness
As you are driving your car, get the feel of your steering wheel and the
seat. Get in touch with your feet touching your shoes. Try to get in
touch with your body.
When you walk be aware of the movement of your legs.
Slow Down
Take one extra minute at breakfast, driving to work, and during other
activities whenever you can. Observe the effect this has on you.
Do One Thing at a Time
Verbalize internally what you are doing as you do it. This will help you
to do one thing at a time.

(c) Exercises for Joy

The Koan
In a medicative environment ask yourself: "What would happen if I let
go of my clinging and negative emotions? What would happen if I let
go of my guilt, my heartbreak, my jealousy, my resentment?" Stay
with this question as long as you can and see what you will discover.

The Awareness: Looking, Hearing, Sensing
Look at some nature scene or some object. Don't look for anything
sensational. Just look as if you are seeing it for the first time.
Listen to all the sounds around you. If possible, avoid putting names to
the sounds. Realize that each sound is really composed of many
sounds. Don't look for anything sensational. Just listen to those
sounds as if you are hearing them for the first time in your life.

The Exclamation
It is impossible to be grateful and unhappy. In a meditative
environment say to yourself repeatedly, "How lucky I am. How
grateful I am." As you repeat these words recall some of your life's
blessings. Go over all the events that happened yesterday. Be grateful
for all these events. Say, "Thank you. How lucky I was that that
happened to me." When you come to an unpleasant event, consider
the seeds for growth that it contains and be grateful.

The Identification
Put yourself in the place of the paralyzed woman who was described
on the program. Lie on your back and say, "I can do all the loveliest
things in the world. I can have all the loveliest things in the world."
Find out what these loveliest things are. If you discover them, you will
find gratitude and you will find abiding joy.

The Blessing
Recall the words of Juliana of Norwich, "And all shall be well. And all
manner of things shall be well." Think of pleasant and unpleasant

events of the past. At each event say, "It was well. It was well." Think of some present things, things that are happening to you now. Say, "It is well. It is well." Think of something coming in the future. Say, "It will be well. It will be well." Your faith will be changed into joy.

(d) Exercises for Freedom

Meditatively imagine what existed one hundred years ago on the spot where you are. What existed there three thousand years ago? What will exist there three thousand years from now?
As a result of this exercise, you will begin to experience a sense of vastness. You will gain a realization that, except in the eyes of God, you are not important.

Good-Bye Exercise
Think of some people you have loved in the past but who are no longer with you. Talk to these people. Say something like, "How lucky I was that you came into my life. How grateful I am to you. And now good-bye. I must go because if I cling to you I will not learn to love the present or the people I am with, so good-bye." Then move to pleasant experiences you have had and personalize them. Repeat the same sequence as above to them. Think of some of your former personal possessions such as your youth or your strength. Personalize them and then repeat the above sequence to them.

Exercise to be Free of Fear
Speak to some fear you have about the future of yours. Then speak to the Lord and thank the Lord in advance for the outcome of the thing you fear.

Exercise to be Free of Ambition
Stand in front of the Lord and make an act of faith to him. Tell him, "Lord, I trust that you are in control of the future. I'm going to do everything in my power to make my dreams come true but I leave the result in your hands." Then imagine that you let go of your ambition. Thank the Lord in advance for the outcome.

(e) Exercises for Creative Love – I have found these exercises very helpful when advising penitents in the Sacrament of Reconciliation.

Talk to Someone You Like
In a meditative environment think of someone you love. Imagine that person is sitting in front of you. Talk to that person. Talk lovingly, describing what that person means to you. As you do this be in touch with what you are feeling.

Talk to Someone You Do Not Like
In the same manner as above think of someone you don't particularly like. Imagine that person is in front of you. As you look at that person, try to see something good in him or her.

See Jesus Look at This Person
Imagine Jesus is standing beside you and he is looking at that person that you do not like.
Jesus becomes your teacher in the art of love. What good and what beauty would Jesus detect in that person? Say what Jesus wold say to that person.

See Jesus Look at You
Imagine you have Jesus in front of you and he tells you all the goodness, the beauty, and all the lovely qualities he sees in you. Don't shirk this exercise. Jesus makes allowances for defects and will see through them to your goodness. What name or names do you think Jesus would make up for you?

Look and Listen
Repeat the first looking exercise of these programs. That is, look at some scene or some object without thinking about it. Don't look for anything sensational. Just look and listen and touch with a quiet mind.

Finally, under this section I would include William Barclay's series of books and commentaries on the New Testament. They have been a great help in preparing talks and homilies, being a readable blend of exegesis, background information and spirituality.

Chapter 6

The Cross and Resurrection

"From then onwards Jesus began to make it clear to his disciples that he was destined to go to Jerusalem and suffer grievously at the hands of the elders and chief priests and scribes, and to be put to death and to be raised up on the third day" (Matthew 16 vs 21)

This penultimate chapter I have headed "Death and Resurrection" as this is the inner pattern of all our lives, and shows so clearly in the way we love and live. I have included also in this chapter a few words about ageing and hospitality, both of which involve a death to self but an experience of new life. It was brought home to me when, some years ago I was diagnosed with aggressive (a horrible word) prostate cancer. However this was happily dealt with after a course of radio therapy. Then more recently, I have had to have treatment for Parkinson's disease, which involves tablets and regular exercise, the latter at which I am not so good.

On a more serious note one of the most amazing books that I have ever read is "The Diving Bell and the Butterfly" by Jean-Dominique Bauby. The author is a man who became completely paralysed by a massive stroke and who wrote by means of flickering one eyelid. On the book cover it tells us that "he produced a work so unusual, moving and beautiful, read and admired around the world. With grace and economy, it describes his life before and after the stroke, his continuing imaginative freedom, and how he comes to terms with what has happened. It is a book that illuminates the very business of being alive."

The following account is similarly moving. It began with Barbara, a visitor to St. Aidan's parish, introducing herself to me, having come on a short visit from the States to see her sister, Pat Billett, who had been diagnosed with MND – "motor neurone disease". Barbara was a practising Catholic and persuaded her sister who had not practised for many years, to come and see me, which she did, together with her non-Catholic husband, Roger. Pat communicated by means of a keyboard on her lap on which she tapped out what she wanted to say, and then by tapping another key one was able to hear a voice speak out. Roger was finding life more difficult than his wife, and was about to negotiate redundancy with the London Underground for whom he worked, so that he could spend as much time as possible with Pat before she died. Pat enjoyed writing poetry and she presented me with a poem she had written recording the stages of her illness in April 2018.

Please take my hand

I have begun a peculiar journey, which I didn't expect to take
A very difficult one I have to say and one I rather not make.

For life has thrown a terrible fate by casting MND on me
But the key to getting through all this, is to take the opportunity that be.

My husband is there all the time, my protector to the end
My family are all there for me, no matter where they live, me they will fend.

My in-laws also have a say, to support us when we ask
I know they do care very much, their concern they try to mask.

Our friends want to help us as much as they can, to ease the burden on us
We can call on them at any time, they will be here without a fuss.

The great people I work with past and present, all share the same concern
Anything they can do to help, about my journey they want to learn.

The wonderful people at Amersham Hospital, so very patient and very kind
Trying all sorts of ways, to give us peace of mind.

The volunteers from MNDA, were quick to offer support
Will be nice to meet with them again, and go through any thoughts.

I have met the priest at the local church, long time overdue
A very endearing and gentle man, it was something I had to do.

I honestly feel quite brave so far, one day at a time I must take
I have so much support to see me through, all the difference it does make.

Don't be frightened, don't be scared, I am carrying on as norm
I'm focusing on the positive, and on the calm before the storm.

I do not know, what lies ahead, it is different for each and every one
It may not be that bad for me, whilst I can, I will still have fun.

So please take my hand, I'd like you to, we can do and share so much
Life continues in a different form, but can still remain in touch.

I have known Caroline Loftus during my time in Northampton. She was always a thoughtful and caring person and when I became involved with the Missionaries of the Poor in Jamaica, she expressed a wish to go to Kingston to help the Brothers in their work for the homeless and destitute. Eventually she made two visits there and got to know the Community well.

Because of her financial experience she then took on the task of being treasurer of our support group, and later became friendly with Dan Richards, also a very caring person, and whom she eventually married. After a comparatively short time Dan contracted cancer and died, but weeks before his death in March 2018, he set down his reflections on his illness. These we found deeply moving and it is appropriate to include some of them here.

> "In Genesis Chapter 3 Verse 6 we read "The Lord said, "My Spirit will not contend with man for ever, for he is mortal, his days will be 120 years". With all medical advances and thousands of years, this remains true as a maximum and is all our own body cells can stand.
> Going on to Psalm 90 verse 10, we read the familiar – three score years and ten – with the possibility of extending it to 80 – but only with care and feeling more pain.
>
> For me to have to die before either of these is, of course, something I desperately tried to avoid. It could have been worse in different circumstances. To be killed in a needless war, by a drunk driver, or a mining disaster, all common tragic events, would be far worse.
>
> It took illness to make me realise what a good wife I had. Weekends away and short breaks became so much more enjoyable. Many interesting cities are a short train journey away. We saw countless museums, galleries, and places we never knew existed. We joined the History Housing Association, a way to see some of the lesser known castles and manor houses, often meeting the owners!

The probability of death improved the quality of my life, and every spring day and every beautiful garden, had more power over me. When I wanted to forget I was ill, I only had to get in touch with Caroline's brother Mick and go to the Errigal yard. Very few small employers would have saved me part-time lighter duties, like they did. I could go off in a van collecting road signs or cleaning up stones on a grass verge and I was a workman again, NOT a patient.

I spoke to Caroline about my wish not to tell people the stage the cancer was at when it was first diagnosed. From the start, all treatment was to be palliative. Not a word I had wanted to hear. The first treatment worked excellently, so much so the doctor told me that I was a miracle, when we explained I was hoping for one! I was so glad none of the awful symptoms they were told me were likely, arose. I did not want to hear the news that the cancer had spread but, all along, I had also been using herbal remedies recommended by other sufferers and I am sure they helped my good response to the chemo. I now added CBD oil, a cannabis based legal product, which certainly helped with sleep and well-being.

My last year was my best year, I remember the good moments so clearly and learnt to relax. When my Carillion shares fell to nothing, instead of being enraged, I just reminded myself it was not that important. Small pleasures in life and people, rather than consumerism, can lead to a happier life. I had been gradually evolving from my 20s, where I thought money was everything, to a sensible middle aged feeling that my priorities had changed. This speed up dramatically as I became ill and I found that quality of life is not measured by wages or a make of car. Some people adapt the other way – old people going to court over fences that are an inch over the boundary and mean farmers closing paths with barbed wire. At times like these, remember the saying "life is too short". Learn to enjoy simple pleasures and don't go through years like I did; once working twelve hours shifts to buy a house and having nothing to remember.

What did I do in 1998? I know where I lived and where I worked and that is all; not a single good memory or even news event from that year do I remember. My last year on earth was the opposite and how much better I felt. I share these experiences to give people an insight into how it feels to be called "palliative" and, may be, how to be when they meet a person who is in my situation. "

Father Bede Griffiths, liked to think of human life in three stages: the first 20 years are the stage of adolescence, the growth in physical maturity; the next 20 years are that of psychological and mental maturity; and the third stage begins in the 40s which is when the spiritual powers begin to awaken and we go beyond space and time. So old age then becomes the flowering of the whole personality. This means that we are not fully human persons until we enter this third stage and we can see ourselves and the whole of existence in a new way. Old age is therefore not a decline, but a fulfilment of our lives. I would add that this means that suffering caused by the breakdown of any or all of these stages should be caught up in anticipation of resurrection and new life.

On a lighter note, it has been said that the secret of staying young is to live honestly, eat slowly, and lie about your age; or as my father, who lived to be nearly a hundred, used to claim, the secret of long life is punctuality, regularity and moderation in all things. During my thirteen years at Northampton Cathedral I used regularly to spend a few days each month with an ecumenical community at Hengrave Hall, near Bury St Edmonds. Soon after I moved to Little Chalfont, one of the temporary members of the community, a Hungarian, came to stay with me for a short time whilst he followed an English language course in London. The "short time" extended to nearly twenty years during which time he, Imre, took up work as a local postman and became a good friend and companion in an otherwise empty presbytery and it has been partly through his willingness to help and cheerful presence that I have been able to continue my vocation into old age.

Murano is one of the small islands off the mainland of Venice. I was told that one need not bother visiting it as it was just full of glassworks. However, this is not true. It is an attractive island and one of its glories is the Church of Santa Maria and Donato, set in an attractive canalside piazza. It is a Romanesque church and in the apse behind the altar there is an unusual Byzantine mosaic of Our Lady. Her hands are strange with palms facing outwards as if trying to ward one off, and she is looking half to one side, as if to say, "not yet".

A few years later I encountered another rather different meeting with Our Lady. It was on the first of several visits to Ephesus. I had taken a taxi to the top of Mount Koressos just outside the ruins of Ephesus to the chapel marking Mary's house. A Muslim lady and her family travelled with me and she explained that Muslims have a great devotion to Mary as the Mother of Jesus, who is considered to be one of the prophets.

On arriving at Mary's house we read how early in the nineteenth century a German nun, Anna Catherine Emmerich, belonging to an enclosed order and who had never been out of Germany, had a vision of a long-buried and forgotten house. She located it accurately and, following her directions, the area was excavated and the foundations of the house were found. In her vision it was revealed to her that it was Mary's house where she had lived. A chapel was built on the foundations and it has since been declared by the Church as a place of pilgrimage.

On later visits I came to know the Franciscan priest Father Tarcy Mathias OFM Cap, who looked after the shrine and the following is taken from a leaflet he wrote.

MERYEM ANA EVI
HOUSE OF THE BLESSED VIRGIN MARY

More than a million visitors a year are said to come to the
shrine of Meryem Ana Evi, the House of Mother Mary near
Ephesus in Turkey. In official documents of the government,
the site is referred to as a museum or a monument. To the
visitors – whatever be their nationalities, cultures, languages,
or religions – it is a sacred place, sacred in the basic and
fundamental religious sense of the word.

Not infrequently, one sees a person – man or woman, young
or old – deeply moved emotionally, very often in tears. One
feels like asking, "Why are you weeping? Are you sad?" The
answer comes: "No, I am not sad; I feel greatly touched; I feel
something special, a peace, joy, a warm welcome, a
happiness. I feel like staying." Others say, "This is a special
place. I feel the presence of Mary, our Mother. She has
certainly lived here."

Perhaps these remarks of many visitors – authentic, sincere,
honest, true and loving are the greatest proof that Mary, the
mother of Jesus, lived the last days of her life here, that she
"died" here like all the rest of us, and that the Assumption
happened here. Mary, the cosmic and universal Mother, is
present here in a very special way.

There are two traditions concerning the last years of Mary's life. Some
say that she came to Ephesus with St. John, but then returned to
Jerusalem and died here. The far greater weight of belief, however, is
that Mary lived the last years of her life in the house built for her by St.
John on the hills near the ancient city of Ephesus. She lived silently
and in prayer, but always ready to help as a Mother. She is believed to
have died in Ephesus and that the Assumption took place here.

Death and the next life reminds me of the following story (origin unknown):

A sick man turned to his doctor as he was preparing to leave the examination room and said, 'Doctor, I am afraid to die, tell me what lies on the other side.' Very quietly, the doctor said, 'I don't know...' 'You don't know? You're a Christian man, and don't know what's on the other side?'
The doctor was holding the handle of the door; on the other side came a sound of scratching and whining, and as he opened the door, a dog sprang into the room and leaped on him with an eager show of gladness. Turning to the patient, the doctor said, 'Did you notice my dog? He's never been in this room before. He didn't know what was inside. He knew nothing except that his master was here, and when the door opened he sprang in without fear. I know little of what is on the other side of death, but I do know one thing.....
I know my master is there and that is enough.'

Chapter 7

Conclusion

Two monks were conversing, and one remarked to the other: "I work, I pray, I fast, but what else should I do?" His companion held up his hand with his fingers stretched out like ten lamps of fire and he said: "If you will you can become all flame."

Coming to the end of these meandering notes in which I have written in some detail of a number of people who have influenced me, I am, nevertheless, fully aware that there are countless others who have helped me in so many different ways and to whom I am eternally grateful.

We live in an age of great change. This applies to the Church, and we have, as I write, a leader in Pope Francis who is well aware of this. He writes in the closing chapter of his "Apostolic Exhortation" on young people:

> "Dear young people, my joyful hope is to see you keep running the race before you, outstripping all those who are slow or fearful, attracted by the face of Christ, whom we love so much, whom we adore in the Holy Eucharist and acknowledge in the flesh of our suffering brothers and sisters. May the Holy Spirit urge you on as you run the race. The Church needs your momentum, your intuitions, your faith. We need them! And when you arrive where we have not yet reached, have the patience to wait for us."

I have tried to show that God is present in all that is beautiful, in bread and wine that is changed into the presence of Christ himself in the Mass, in people who are suffering, indeed, in all of us, and in God's Word in the Scriptures, in art, music, drama and sculpture. I began these memoirs by describing a fire. There is a Catholic prayer which reads "Come Holy Spirit, fill the hearts of your faithful and kindle in them the fire of your love". I have tried to show how the fire of love, the power of the Holy Spirit, has been clearly present in so many people who have come into my life. My prayer is that you, the reader, may also be inspired. Everything is summed up in our belief in God, the Trinity, an essential but very misunderstood, article of our Christian faith, and it is on this note that I would like to conclude.

The inspiration for much of what follows was found in Dorothy Sayer's book "The Mind of the Maker", first published in 1941, and I am grateful to her - a remarkable Anglican theologian who is, nevertheless, known more for her plays and detective stories than for her theology. In her play "The Zeal of my House" she writes: "For every work (or act) of creation is threefold, an earthly trinity to match the heavenly. First, (not in time, but merely in order of enumeration) there is the Creative idea, passionless, timeless, beholding the whole work complete at once, the end in the beginning; and this is the image of the Father. Second, there is the Creative energy (or Activity) begotten of that idea, working in time from beginning to end, with sweat and passion, being incarnate in the bonds of matter: and this is the image of the Word. Third, there is the Creative power, the meaning of the work and its response in the lively soul: and this is the image of the indwelling Spirit." And these three are one, each equally in itself the whole work, whereof none can exist without the other: and this is the image of the Trinity." And this is inspired by the words I once read, "when we become creative we approach holiness, wholeness – love". In her book "The Mind of the Maker", she expands on this theme and takes as her main example the mind of the writer of a book. The idea of a book is there in the author's mind; it then becomes "incarnate", readable, seeable, touchable; and, if the work has been well done, we can say that the author loves this "incarnation" of his or her idea. These three aspects of the human work of creation are an image, albeit an imperfect one, of the heavenly Trinity.

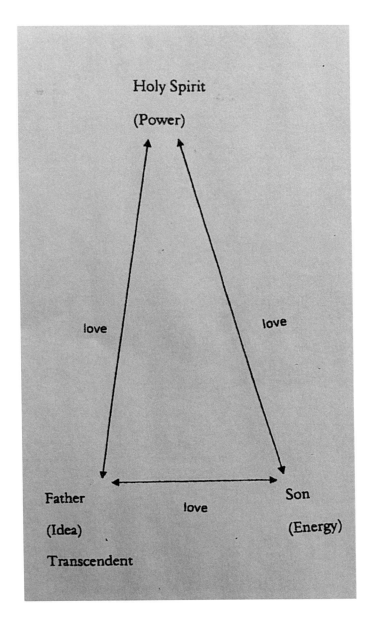

St. Augustine wrote:

> "The image of the Trinity was made in man that in this way man should be the image of the one true God." Personally, I prefer the example of the artist who is painting a landscape. If he is really a good artist he will think first of the picture he wants to paint and will decide how to paint the lake, the background of trees and shadows, the boat on the lake and the fisherman. All this will be in his mind and he may tell his friends that he is going to paint a picture and describe it to them. They then will have some idea of what it is going to be like. He then sets about putting his idea on canvas. When completed, his friends will, he hopes, admire it, like it, love it, and say, "Ah, now we can see what you were describing to us: we can see the idea that was in your mind.""

Here then, we have a clear Trinitarian image: the idea of the painting, and image of God, the Father; the approximate description of that idea before it becomes something tangible, is like the revelation of God to people before the coming of Christ, and the actual painting when completed, is an image of God, the Son, incarnation of the Father; and, finally the appreciation and love the artist and others have for the painting is an image of the Holy Spirit of love.

An even better Trinitarian image is found in the act of love between husband and wife. There is first of all, thought – perhaps sometimes an almost unconscious desire – on the part of the two people, which through intercourse, the act of love proceeding from each of them, may result in a third person. In this example we have a better image of the third "person" of the heavenly Trinity.

However, this expression of love or image of the Trinity in our relationships is not limited. It is found, or should be, in our relationships with one another. St. Augustine said, "If you see love, you see the Trinity", or "Where there is love, there is God." The heart of the Trinity is love and the heart of love is the Trinity.

In God of course, we are speaking of perfection. The first "Person" of the Trinity utters his Word and externalises his thought and this is the Second Person of the Trinity, and they are bound for all time to each other by Love, the Holy Spirit. Here, we must always bear in mind that the word "Person" is not used in the Trinity in the way in which we normally use it.

However, not only do we find this trinitarian image in human acts of love and creation, but, to a lesser degree, in all our acts. Before we do anything there is the thought, the idea of doing it. It may be passing the salt at the dinner table or cleaning one's teeth or driving the car. The thought then becomes an action, it becomes incarnate, something seeable that can be experienced, the activity or energy. Then thirdly if we have acted well, there is the satisfaction, the love, the power between the thought and the action.

Many of the great saints have said that the smallest act done with love is of infinite value. Why is this? Simply, as we have just seen, it becomes a reflexion of the Trinity, and through it we are caught up in the movement of love that is God. I think it was Saint Teresa of Calcutta who remarked that we can do no great things – only small things with great love.

This, I would hasten to emphasise, is only an imperfect image of the heavenly Trinity, where time does not exist and so all three exist simultaneously. The Son is begotten of the Father from all time, before time began, and the two are bound together in the fire of love, the Holy Spirit.

Loving encounters are friendships that have caught fire. So may we all be caught up in this fire of love.

Spreading the Good News through books by Fr Kenneth Payne

Stretch Out Your Hand
The Catholic faith for those who are searching

Shades of Welcome
Personal experiences of the importance of hospitality

What Shall I Say? (Columba Press)
Homily Suggestions covering Catholic teaching for the three year cycle of readings

Central Line to Eziat
Thought provoking fiction, on the Christian theme of providence.

Thoughts, Anecdotes and Stories from a Priest's Notebook
Prayerful, amusing and revelatory

Joy for All?
The story of Father Richard Ho Lung, founder of the Missionaries of the Poor

The Rosary for Today (McCrimmons Press)
Meaningful ways of saying the Rosary

Questions Children Ask, With Possible Answers (McCrimmons Press)
Useful for parents, teachers and even grandparents!

Did they laugh?
Highlighting some of the amusing passages in the Gospels

Edited by Fr Kenneth Payne

It's been a Good Life
Amusing memoirs of the long, eventful and unusual life of Ian Ainsley, professional actor, artist and tour guide.

Love Will Overcome
An enlivening selection from the writings, retreats and conferences of Fr Henri Boulad, S.J.

The Challenge of Brazil
Lay leadership in the Church recounted by Sister Katey Dougan's mission in Brazil

Copies of these books may be obtained (postage free) from

St Aidan's, Finch Lane, Little Chalfont, Bucks, HP7 9NE or from www.amazon.co.uk

WS - #0219 - 121222 - C0 - 197/132/4 - PB - 9781784567040 - Gloss Lamination